MW01713939

**STUDY GUIDE**

Jerome Kodell, O.S.B.

LITTLE ROCK SCRIPTURE STUDY

*A ministry of the Diocese of Little Rock*
*in partnership with Liturgical Press*

DIOCESE OF LITTLE ROCK

2500 North Tyler Street • P.O. Box 7239 • Little Rock, Arkansas 72217 • (501) 664-0340 • Fax (501) 664-6304

Office of the Bishop

Dear Friends in Christ,

The Bible comes to us as both a gift and an opportunity. It is a gift of God who loves us enough to communicate with us. The only way to enjoy the gift is to open and savor it. The Bible is also an opportunity to actually meet God who is present in the stories, teachings, people, and prayers that fill its pages.

I encourage you to open your Bibles in anticipation that God will do something good in your life. I encourage you to take advantage of the opportunity to meet God in prayer, study, and small-group discussion.

Little Rock Scripture Study offers materials that are simple to use, and a method that has been tested by time. The questions in this study guide will direct your study, help you to understand the passages you are reading, and challenge you to relate the Scriptures to your own life experiences.

Allow the Word of God to form you as a disciple of the Lord Jesus. Accept the challenge to be "transformed by the renewal of your mind" (Romans 12:2). Above all, receive God's Word as his gift, and act upon it.

Sincerely in Christ,

+ J. Peter Sartain

✠ J. Peter Sartain
Bishop of Little Rock

# *Sacred Scripture*

"The Church has always venerated the divine Scriptures just as she venerates the body of the Lord, since from the table of both the word of God and of the body of Christ she unceasingly receives and offers to the faithful the bread of life, especially in the sacred liturgy. She has always regarded the Scriptures together with sacred tradition as the supreme rule of faith, and will ever do so. For, inspired by God and committed once and for all to writing, they impart the word of God Himself without change, and make the voice of the Holy Spirit resound in the words of the prophets and apostles. Therefore, like the Christian religion itself, all the preaching of the Church must be nourished and ruled by sacred Scripture. For in the sacred books, the Father who is in heaven meets His children with great love and speaks with them; and the force and power in the word of God is so great that it remains the support and energy of the Church, the strength of faith for her sons, the food of the soul, the pure and perennial source of spiritual life."

Vatican II, Dogmatic Constitution on Divine Revelation, no. 21.

## INTERPRETATION OF SACRED SCRIPTURE

"Since God speaks in sacred Scripture through men in human fashion, the interpreter of sacred Scripture, in order to see clearly what God wanted to communicate to us, should carefully investigate what meaning the sacred writers really intended, and what God wanted to manifest by means of their words.

"Those who search out the intention of the sacred writers must, among other things, have regard for 'literary forms.' For truth is proposed and expressed in a variety of ways, depending on whether a text is history of one kind or another, or whether its form is that of prophecy, poetry, or some other type of speech. The interpreter must investigate what meaning the sacred writer intended to express and actually expressed in particular circumstances as he used contemporary literary forms in accordance with the situation of his own time and culture. For the correct understanding of what the sacred author wanted to assert, due attention must be paid to the customary and characteristic styles of perceiving, speaking, and narrating which prevailed at the

time of the sacred writer, and to the customs men normally followed at that period in their everyday dealings with one another."
Vatican II, Dogmatic Constitution on Divine Revelation, no. 12.

# *Instructions*

## MATERIALS FOR THE STUDY

**This Study Guide:** Exodus

**Bible:** The New American Bible with Revised New Testament or The New Jerusalem Bible is recommended. Paraphrased editions are discouraged as they offer little if any help when facing difficult textual questions. Choose a Bible you feel free to write in or underline.

**Commentary:** *The God of Freedom and Life* by Stephen J. Binz (The Liturgical Press) is used with this study. The assigned pages are found at the beginning of each lesson.

## ADDITIONAL MATERIALS

**Bible Dictionary:** *The Dictionary of the Bible* by John L. McKenzie (Simon & Schuster) is highly recommended as an additional reference.

**Notebook:** A notebook may be useful for lecture notes and your personal reflections.

## WEEKLY LESSONS

Lesson 1—Exod 1–3
Lesson 2—Exod 4:1–6:27
Lesson 3—Exod 6:28–10:29
Lesson 4—Exod 11–12
Lesson 5—Exod 13–15
Lesson 6—Exod 16–18
Lesson 7—Exod 19–24
Lesson 8—Exod 25–31
Lesson 9—Exod 32–40

## YOUR DAILY PERSONAL STUDY

The first step is prayer. Open your heart and mind to God. Reading Scripture is an opportunity to listen to God who loves you.

Pray that the same Holy Spirit who guided the formation of Scripture will inspire you to correctly understand what you read and empower you to make what you read a part of your life.

The next step is commitment. Daily spiritual food is as necessary as food for the body. This study is divided into daily units. Schedule a regular time and place for your study, as free from distractions as possible. Allow about twenty minutes a day. Make it a daily appointment with God.

As you begin each lesson read the assigned chapters of Scripture found at the beginning of each lesson, the footnotes in your Bible, and then the indicated pages of the commentary. This preparation will give you an overview of the entire lesson and help you to appreciate the context of individual passages.

As you reflect on Scripture, ask yourself these four questions:

1. *What does the Scripture passage say?*
   Read the passage slowly and reflectively. Use your imagination to picture the scene or enter into it.
2. *What does the Scripture passage mean?*
   Read the footnotes and the commentary to help you understand what the sacred writers intended and what God wanted to communicate by means of their words.
3. *What does the Scripture passage mean to me?*
   Meditate on the passage. God's Word is living and powerful. What is God saying to you today? How does the Scripture passage apply to your life today?
4. *What am I going to do about it?*
   Try to discover how God may be challenging you in this passage. An encounter with God contains a challenge to know God's will and follow it more closely in daily life.

## THE QUESTIONS ASSIGNED FOR EACH DAY

Read the questions and references for each day. The questions are designed to help you listen to God's Word and to prepare you for the weekly small-group discussion.

Some of the questions can be answered briefly and objectively by referring to the Bible references and the commentary *(What does the passage say?).* Some will lead you to a better understanding of how the Scriptures apply to the Church, sacraments, and society *(What does the passage mean?).* Some questions will invite you to consider how God's Word challenges or supports you in your relationships with God and others *(What does the passage mean to me?).* Finally, the questions will lead you to examine your actions in light of Scripture *(What am I going to do about it?).*

Write your responses in this study guide or in a notebook to help you clarify and organize your thoughts and feelings.

## THE WEEKLY SMALL-GROUP MEETING

The weekly small-group sharing is the heart of the Little Rock Scripture Study Program. Participants gather in small groups to share the results of praying, reading and reflecting on Scripture and on the assigned questions. The goal of the discussion is for group members to be strengthened and nourished individually and as a community through sharing how God's Word speaks to them and affects their daily lives. The daily study questions will guide the discussion; it is not necessary to discuss all the questions.

All members share the responsibility of creating an atmosphere of loving support and trust in the group by respecting the opinions and experiences of others, and by affirming and encouraging one another. The simple shared prayer which begins and ends each small group meeting also helps create the open and trusting environment in which group members can share their faith deeply and grow in the study of God's Word.

A distinctive feature of this program is its emphasis on and trust in God's presence working in and through each member. Sharing responses to God's presence in the Word and in others can bring about remarkable growth and transformation.

## THE WRAP-UP LECTURE

The lecture is designed to develop and clarify the themes of the lesson. It is not intended to form the basis for the group discussion. For this reason the lecture is always held at the end of the meeting. If several small groups meet at one time, the large group will gather together in a central location to listen to the lecture.

Lectures may be given by a local speaker. They are also available on audio- or video-cassette.

# LESSON 1 Exod 1–3

## The God of Freedom and Life, pages 7–23

**Day 1**

1. What do you hope to receive in this study of the Book of Exodus?
2. Why is the Book of Exodus considered central to the faith of both Jews and Christians? (See commentary.)
3. a) What evidence have scholars found to indicate that Exodus is a combination of several traditions?
   b) How might this understanding enrich your study of Exodus?

**Day 2**

4. How had Israel come to be enslaved in Egypt (1:1-10)? (See Gen 46–47.)
5. What kinds of slavery chain people today? (See John 8:34; Rom 6:16; Titus 3:3.)
6. The king sought an easy solution to Egypt's problems (1:8-16, 22). Give examples of how we do this today.

**Day 3**

7. a) Like the Hebrew midwives, what pressures do you experience to do wrong (1:15-16)?
   b) How were the midwives able to know good from evil, and choose goodness (1:17, 21)? (See Ps 19:8-11; Prov 1:7; 8:13.)
8. How would you describe the difference between Pharaoh's attitude to life and that of the women in the story (1:17–2:10)?
9. What is the significance of Moses' name (2:10)?

**Day 4**

10. What similarities are there between Moses' infancy and that of Jesus in Matthew 2:19-21?

11. What does the episode in 2:11-12 reveal to you about Moses? (See Acts 7:23-24.)

12. Moses was well cared for after his crisis in Egypt (2:20-22). Can you describe a time of divine providence in your life?

**Day 5**

13. Moses named his son "Gershom" (2:22).
    a) When would this name have a spiritual significance for the Israelites? (See Num 32:13; Hos 9:17.)
    b) What is its significance for Christians? (See Heb 13:14.)

14. Why do you think God's own people had to wait so long for deliverance (2:23-24)? (See Luke 21:12-19; 2 Thess 1:4-5.)

15. a) What was Moses' age when he experienced God's call (3:1-3)? (See 7:7; Acts 7:23, 30.)
    b) Describe a time in your life when you had a "burning bush" experience, an encounter with God.

**Day 6**

16. a) Why was Moses afraid to look at God (3:6)? (See 1 Kgs 19:11-13.)
    b) Have you ever been fearful of the Lord's calling? (See Ps 139:1-18.)

17. God promises Moses, "I will be with you" (3:12). Is this sufficient for our trials also? (See Josh 1:5; Jer 15:20; Matt 1:23; 28:20.)

18. What does the divine name reveal about God (3:13-14)? (See John 8:58.)

# LESSON 2 Exod 4:1–6:27

## The God of Freedom and Life, pages 23–33

**Day 1**

1. What did you learn about Moses from last week's discussion or lecture?
2. Why was Moses so reluctant to accept God's mission for him (3:11, 13; 4:1, 10, 13)? (See Jer 1:4-6.)
3. What is the significance of the three signs given to Moses (4:1-9)? (See 7:10, 17.)

**Day 2**

4. Moses is afraid he will not be able to speak (4:10-11).
   a) What is Jesus' assurance to Christians who feel inadequate or unable to speak about their faith? (See Matt 10:19-20; Luke 12:11-12; John 15:26.)
   b) When have you felt God's help in saying the right thing at the right time?
5. God's chosen leaders are sometimes called to act without knowing the full plan (4:13). Why is this so? (See Gen 12:1-5; Isa 55:8-9; Heb 11:23-29.)
6. How does God respond to Moses' lack of ability (4:10-15)? (See 7:1-2.)

**Day 3**

7. Moses makes a physical journey back to Egypt (4:19-31). In what sense is this also a spiritual journey?
8. To whom do Moses and Aaron first announce deliverance (4:29-31)?
9. a) How would you describe Pharaoh's response to God's command "Let my people go" (5:1-2)?
   b) In our world today, where do you see this struggle repeated between God and those in political power?

**Day 4**

10. How is the faith of the people tested (5:6-9)?

11. a) Put yourself in Moses' position. What anguish might he have been feeling after Pharaoh's response (5:22-23)?
    b) Do you address God with such honesty? Why or why not?

12. Recall a time when you experienced a setback in your plans. How were you able to persevere?

**Day 5**

13. List the promises God makes to the people in 6:1-8.

14. a) What prevented the Israelites from hearing God's promises (6:9)?
    b) When have you seen something similar happen? (See Num 21:4-5; Ps 78:40-42; Mark 14:32-42, 66-72.)

15. If the "heart of the covenant" is expressed in 6:7, as the commentary suggests, how would you define covenant?

**Day 6**

16. What is the purpose of the genealogy found in 6:14-25? (See 32:29; Deut 18:1-2.)

17. Moses was raised as an Egyptian. Why emphasize his ethnic roots at this point in the story?

# LESSON 3 Exod 6:28–10:29

## The God of Freedom and Life, pages 33–47

**Day 1**

1. What is one insight you would like to remember from last week's lecture?
2. What is God's purpose in making Pharaoh obstinate (7:3)? (See Exod 7-8; Rom 9:18.)
3. For the Hebrews, the heart was the seat of one's will, intellect, and emotions. What does it mean to be hard of heart (7:3, 14)? (See Matt 13:13-15; Mark 3:4-5; Heb 3:12-14.)

**Day 2**

4. What was the purpose of the plagues (7:14–11:10)? (See Ps 105:26-38.)
5. Jesus said miracles will not convince those who don't want to be convinced (Luke 16:31).
   a) Give an example from the ministry of Jesus where a miracle received conflicting responses.
   b) Are miracles necessary for faith?
6. Some of the plagues may have been intensified natural occurrences in Egypt (e.g., hailstorms, locust swarms). Does this mean that God did not cause the plagues? (See Luke 5:1-11.)

**Day 3**

7. a) Why did Pharaoh request the prayers of Moses and Aaron (8:1-7)?
   b) What situations have caused you to request the prayers of others? (See Rom 15:30-31; Col 4:2-4; Jas 5:16.)
8. Which of the plagues might have been most convincing of God's power for you? Why?
9. What force in the world today would you identify as the greatest block to God's work? Why? (See 9:17.)

**Day 4**

10. Are natural disasters such as floods and tornadoes a punishment from God (9:22-26)? (See Matt 5:44-45; Luke 13:1-5.)

11. Describe a natural event that heightened your awareness of God as master of creation.

12. Pharaoh seems to acknowledge his sin, but then returns to his old ways (9:27, 34-35).
    a) What caused his confession?
    b) How can we know if our own confession of sin is sincere? (See Ps 51:1-19; Prov 28:13; 1 John 1:9-10.)

**Day 5**

13. Moses refuses to accept a compromise, insisting that all Israel must be allowed to worship God (10:17). Can someone else worship in your place? (See 1 Chr 16:28-29; Ps 63:2-9.)

14. Why is the participation of all so vital to the celebration of the Eucharist? (See 1 Cor 10:17.)

15. When prevented by force or illness from public worship (see 8:21-23), what alternatives does one have to express faith and praise to God?

**Day 6**

16. Consider your own experiences of darkness. What do you think God communicated by sending "dense darkness throughout the land of Egypt" (10:22)? (See Job 10:20-22; Rom 13:12; Eph 5:8-11.)

17. What would be your reaction after nine plagues
    a) if you were an Egyptian?
    b) if you were an Israelite?
    c) if you were Moses?

18. Throughout the account of the plagues, God is said to have made Pharaoh obdurate. Is Pharaoh still responsible for his actions?

# LESSON 4 Exod 11–12

## The God of Freedom and Life, pages 47–55

**Day 1**

1. What did you learn about God's desires for Israel in last week's lesson covering nine of the plagues?
2. What personal qualities and leadership skills did Moses show in his dealings with Pharaoh that would have placed him in high regard among the Egyptians (11:3)? (See Heb 3:1-5; 11:23-29.)
3. Moses left Pharaoh's presence in "hot anger" (11:8). When is anger justified and how might it be used constructively? (See Mark 3:4-5; 11:15; Eph 4:26.)

**Day 2**

4. Why would the month of Abib stand "at the head" of Israel's calendar (12:2)? (See 13:4; 23:15; Deut 16:1.)
5. What are the rules for the Passover Lamb (12:3-10, 46)?
6. How does an understanding of the Passover Lamb help you appreciate Jesus as the Lamb of God? (See Isa 53:7-10; John 1:29; Acts 8:29-35; 1 Cor 5:7; 1 Pet 1:18-19.)

**Day 3**

7. Read 12:11 and comment on how this passage could apply to our lives as Christians. (See Matt 24:36-44; Luke 10:3-4; 1 Thess 5:1-4.)
8. What is the origin of the term "Passover" (12:11-13, 23-27)?
9. How does Israel's deliverance from destruction prefigure our redemption in Christ? (See Wis 18:14-16; Heb 12:22-24; 1 Pet 1:17-19; Rev 19:11-16.)

**Day 4**

10. Why was unleavened bread connected with the Passover (12:14-20)? (See 12:34, 39; 1 Cor 5:7.)
11. What significant uses does hyssop have (12:22)? (See Ps 51:9-11; John 19:28-30; Heb 9:19-20.)
12. The Hebrew child asks about the meaning of the Passover rite (12:26-27).
    a) Describe a family tradition that helps to pass on your faith.
    b) Which part of the Mass explains the meaning of the new Passover in Christ?

**Day 5**

13. Give an example of how the evil done by one generation has far reaching effects on future generations (12:29-30).
14. a) Do the Egyptians fear God because of faith or superstition (12:33)?
    b) How would you describe the difference?
15. Describe an experience you have had of "keeping vigil" (12:42). What lasting lesson have you found in that experience?

**Day 6**

16. What is the significance of circumcision related to the Passover (12:44, 48)?
17. Why is the Passover a communal celebration rather than a private one (12:47)?

# LESSON 5 Exod 13–15

## The God of Freedom and Life, pages 55–64

**Day 1**

1. What idea from last week's discussion or lecture helps you to better understand the importance of the Passover ritual?
2. Why are the "first-born" sons consecrated to the Lord (13:1-2, 11-15)? (See Deut 15:19-23; Luke 2:23.)
3. What physical signs remind you that you also are consecrated to God (13:16)?

**Day 2**

4. a) Why didn't God lead the people directly to the Promised Land by the shortest route (13:17)? (See Num 14:1-4.)
   b) Recall one time in your life when you felt you were wandering. What lesson did you learn from that experience?
5. What was the purpose of the cloud and the fire (13:21-22)? (See 40:34-38; Num 9:15-23; 1 Cor 10:1-3.)
6. On the Christian journey, what forces seem to be in pursuit of God's people (14:8-10)?

**Day 3**

7. a) Describe a time when you second-guessed God's plans for your life (14:10-12).
   b) How did you regain your trust in God?
8. What is the "victory" God will win for the Israelites (14:13)? (See 2 Chr 20:17; Ps 103:2-5.)
9. Recount a specific time in your life when you were sure of God's protection (14:19-20). (See Pss 91:1-7; 121:5-8.)

**Day 4**

10. Where is there evidence that at least two traditions were used to tell the story of crossing the sea (14:16, 21)?

11. How would you describe Israel's journey from fear (14:11-13) to faith-filled trust (14:29-31)? (See Ps 106:6-12.)

12. When have you experienced or witnessed the defeat of the powerful and the victory of the powerless?

**Day 5**

13. Israel responded to God's victory by singing (15:1-21). How have you responded to the triumphs of God in your life?

14. What do you like and dislike about the image of God as a "warrior" (15:3)? (See Isa 9:5-6; 42:13.)

15. a) What is the mountain referred to in 15:17? (See Ps 48:9-12; Isa 2:3; 8:18.)
    b) What is its spiritual meaning? (See Ps 125:1-2; Heb 12:18-23; Rev 14:1-2.)

**Day 6**

16. a) Why did the people still grumble after all God had done (15:22-24)? (See 16:2; 17:1-3.)
    b) Identify a few common grumblings against God today.

17. Compare the meaning of "Passover" in 12:11-12 and in 15:16.

18. List the characteristics of effective leadership you find in Moses in chapters 14 and 15.

# LESSON 6 Exod 16–18

## The God of Freedom and Life, pages 65–73

**Day 1**

1. In the story up to this point, what is your strongest impression of the Israelites?
2. a) What difficult periods of our own history do we tend to glamorize or romanticize (16:3)? (See 5:6-13.)
   b) Why is it important to balance these recollections with an accurate picture of reality?
3. What "desert" experiences have at first seemed impossible, and later proved to be blessings for you (16:3)?

**Day 2**

4. How does the "daily portion" of manna given to Israel (16:4) help you to understand the "daily bread" we pray for in the Lord's Prayer? (See Matt 6:9-15.)
5. How is Jesus the true manna? (See John 6:31-33.)
6. Why were the Israelites instructed not to save manna for the following day (16:19)? (See Matt 6:25-34.)

**Day 3**

7. a) What is the purpose of complete rest on the Sabbath (16:23)? (See 20:10; 31:14-17.)
   b) In what ways does this Sabbath command challenge you personally?
8. The Israelites preserved a portion of the manna for their descendents (16:33), as a reminder of God's providence. What particular sign of God's care could you preserve for future generations in your family?
9. When was the last time you echoed the sentiments of Israel at Massah and Meribah (17:7)? Why?

**Day 4**

10. What similarities do you see between the rock that provided drink (17:6-7) and Jesus, who also provided for those thirsting? (See John 4:7-15; 7:37-39; 19:31-34.)

11. How does Moses' role during the battle foreshadow the role of Jesus on our behalf (17:8-13)? (See Rom 8:34; Heb 4:14–5:3; 1 John 2:1-2.)

12. When have your prayers for others drawn you closer to God? (See Rom 15:30; 1 Tim 2:1-4.)

**Day 5**

13. What role will Joshua play in Israel's history (17:8-13)? (See Num 27:12-23; Josh 1:1-9; 13:1-7.)

14. What pattern in 18:9-12 is similar to that of the Mass? (See 2 Sam 6:17-19; Luke 24:25-30.)

15. a) Why did Moses listen to Jethro, a Midianite priest and non-believer, on a matter of religious authority (18:13-23)?
    b) What could this say about problem-solving in the Church today?

**Day 6**

16. What are some of the ways in which God's will is made known to you (18:16)? (See Matt 23:1-2; Rom 13:1; 1 Cor 2:16.)

17. The growth of a communitv of believers presents problems of authority and organization. Moses faced this problem in 18:13-16; the apostles, in Acts 6:1-6, have the same concern. How are the two solutions similar?

# LESSON 7 Exod 19–24

## The God of Freedom and Life, pages 73–97

**Day 1**

1. What one idea from last week's lecture do you want to remember for your own spiritual growth?
2. God calls Israel "my special possession" (19:5), "a kingdom of priests, a holy nation" (19:16). Which of these descriptions is most meaningful for your relationship with God? (See Num 16:2-3; 1 Pet 2:4-10; Rev 1:5-6.)
3. What are the reasons for the cleansing and prohibitions in 19:9-15, 21-25? (See Isa 6:3-7.)

**Day 2**

4. What is the significance of ascending the mountain (19:20)? (See Gen 22:1-19; Isa 8:18; Matt 14:23; 17:1-5.)
5. Rewrite each of the Ten Commandments in your own words, in a positive way, rather than as prohibitions (20:1-17). Be ready to share these with your group. (See Deut 5:6-21; Matt 5:21-48.)
6. How do the Ten Commandments (20:1-17) correspond to Jesus' commands in Mark 12:28-34? (See Lev 19:17-18; Deut 6:4-5.)

**Day 3**

7. Do the Ten Commandments usually seem like a burden or a gift to you? Why? (See Pss 19:8-11; 119:33-40; Rom 7:19-22.)
8. In what practical ways can we "honor" our parents (20:12)? (See Lev 19:3; Prov 23:22.)
9. What kind of "fear" is induced by God's revelation (20:20)? (See Pss 19:10; 130:3-4; Prov 1:7; 8:13; 14:26-27.)

**Day 4**

10. Slavery was an accepted institution in the ancient world. How does 21:1-11 try to challenge this institution? (See Col 3:22–4:1.)
11. The provisions in 21:12-32 ensure that crime against others does not pay. How does our society promote respect for others?
12. How does Jesus address an over-emphasis on retaliation? (See Matt 5:38-42.)

**Day 5**

13. Treatment of the outcast is addressed in 22:20-23.
    a) Who are the "aliens," "widows," and "orphans" in our midst?
    b) How does your parish directly respond to their needs?
14. God is "compassionate" to the poor (22:26). When has divine compassion challenged you to reach out to another in need?
15. What are the three main feasts for Israelite pilgrimage (23:14-17)? (See John 7:2; Acts 2:1.)

**Day 6**

16. Why was blood sprinkled to ratify the covenant (24:5-8)? (See Lev 17:11; Deut 12:23-28.)
17. How is the covenant blood ritual fulfilled in the New Testament? (See Matt 26:27-28; Heb 9:19-23; 10:29; 1 Pet 1:2.)
18. a) How does the Christian community ratify and renew the new covenant?
    b) How do you continue to renew this covenant as an individual?

# LESSON 8 Exod 25–31

## The God of Freedom and Life, pages 97–119

**Day 1**

1. What is one lesson you learned about the covenant at Sinai from last week's lecture?
2. The materials used to build the Dwelling for Yahweh are collected from the entire people (25:1-8). How do you contribute to creating a space for worship?
3. Why was the Ark of the Covenant so precious to Israel (25:8-10, 22)? (See 2 Sam 6:11-15; Heb 9:1-5.)

**Day 2**

4. Why is Mary sometimes called the new Ark of the Covenant? (See Luke 1:35-45.)
5. What details of the Dwelling have parallels in your parish church (25:10–27:21)?
6. a) Describe a time when physical environment enhanced your experience of worship.
   b) What message is communicated to the congregation by the style of your church building?

**Day 3**

7. How does the description of the Dwelling enrich your appreciation of what it means to actually be a part of God's dwelling yourself? (See 1 Cor 6:15-20; Eph 2:19-22; Col 2:6-7; 1 Pet 2:4-5.)
8. a) Why does Aaron wear the two onyx stones (28:9-12)?
   b) What physical symbol used in the Mass is the most meaningful to you? Why?
9. Why would the instrument of decision-making be worn over the heart (28:29-30)? (See Lev 8:7-8; Sir 45:10-11.)

**Day 4**

10. a) When is anointing with oil (29:7) used in the Church today? (See John 12:1-8; Acts 10:38; 2 Cor 1:21-22; Jas 5:14.)
    b) What does it signify? (See 30:26-32; 1 Sam 10:1; Mark 6:13.)

11. What difference does it make that Jesus is our high priest? (See Heb 2:17-18; 5:7-10; 9:11-15; 10:19-23.)

12. a) What is a "holocaust" (29:18)? (See Lev 1:3-17.)
    b) What new significance does the term have when applied to the slaughter of Jews in this century?

**Day 5**

13. Even after all the sacrifices from the priests, what makes the Dwelling sacred (29:43)?

14. Which title of Jesus is foreshadowed in 29:44-46? (See Ps 46:8; Isa 7:14; Matt 1:22-23.)

15. Why do rich and poor pay the same ransom tax (30:14-16)? (See Matt 17:24-27.)

**Day 6**

16. How does the construction of the Dwelling differ from Israel's earlier works of construction in Egypt (31:1-11)? (See 1:11-14; 5:14-21.)

17. What has God especially gifted you to do, artistic or otherwise (31:1-6)? (See 1 Cor 12:4-7; Eph 4:7.)

18. Commands concerning the Sabbath have been repeated often (20:8-11; 23:10-13; 31:12-18.) Why is there such a strong emphasis on this command?

# LESSON 9 Exod 32–40

## The God of Freedom and Life, pages 119–147

**Day 1**

1. What most impressed you from last week's discussion or lecture?
2. What prompted the Israelites to forget their earlier enthusiastic response to God (32:1-6)? (See 19:8; 24:7-8.)
3. a) When have you experienced the strongest temptation against faith in God's care and guidance?
   b) What spiritual habits or disciplines could anchor you in faithfulness to God?

**Day 2**

4. Israel's disobedience of God's command led to idolatry (32:4-8). Give some modern examples of idolatry in our culture. (See Acts 7:39-41; Phil 3:19-20.)
5. a) Is Moses defending the people's action (32:11-14, 30-34)? (See Deut 9:25-29; Josh 7:6-9; Pss 103:8-13; 106:23.)
   b) How does this scene compare to Jesus' action with the woman caught in adultery (John 8:2-11)? (See Jas 5:16.)
6. How do you reconcile God's wrath (32:10) with God's kindness and mercy (34:6-7)? (See Lam 3:22-23; Rom 2:5-8; 1 Pet 1:3-4.)

**Day 3**

7. List some of the positive and negative examples of spiritual leadership found in Exodus 32.
8. a) Why can't Moses see the face of God (33:18-23)? (See Num 4:20; 1 Tim 6:15-16.)
   b) How does Jesus modify this distance from God? (See John 14:8-10; 2 Cor 3:12-18.)
9. Recall a time of intimate encounter with God. How was God made known to you? (See 1 Cor 12:27.)

**Day 4**

10. Israel understood God's nature as described in 34:6-7. Based on your experiences, what would you include in a description of God? (See 1 John 3:2.)

11. What is implied about Moses' relationship with God by the radiance of his face (34:27-35)?

12. Chapters 35–40 repeat much of the information from earlier chapters of Exodus (25–31). Why? (See 39:32.)

**Day 5**

13. The anointing spoken of in 40:9 served to remind Israel that the Dwelling was sacred. Describe any anointing of a structure that you have witnessed. What difference did it make?

14. Discuss the pros and cons of hereditary priesthood (40:12-15).

15. The fire and cloud were signs of God's care and guidance of God's people. What serves as cloud and fire in your life?

**Day 6**

16. The Book of Exodus records the relationship between God and Israel. What title would you create for the story?

17. Every life is a story of Exodus. Where are you in the Exodus: in slavery in Egypt, on the Egypt side of the sea afraid to cross, crossing, on the other side looking back, murmuring in the desert, or faithful in the desert?

18. In what practical ways can you incorporate the message of freedom and life in your dealings with people?

# NOTES